D1601721

Prayers from a
Wounded Warrior

Prayers from a Wounded Warrior

Laura Barnhart

Photos Credits: Laura Barnhart, Martha Benn, Lynn Ellen Doxon, John Freshnock, Robert Habiger, and Jennifer Wilson

Artemesia Publishing
Rocky Mount, North Carolina

Artemesia Publishing
PO Box 6508
Rocky Mount, NC
252-985-2877
info@artemesiapublishing.com
www.artemesiapublising.com

Library of Congress Cataloging-in-Publication Data

Barnhart, Laura
        Prayers from a wounded warrior./by Laura Barnhart
        p. cm.
        ISBN 1-932926-31-3
        LCCN: 2004111037

First printing

This book is lovingly dedicated to Diana Statzula, more than words can ever say.

ACKNOWLEDGEMENTS

Cindy Borg, for twenty years we have traversed mountains and walked through valleys.

Jennifer Wilson, she gave wings to my prayers.

Kathy Barnhart, she has a heart of gold.

Marianne Williamson opened the door. She made me believe in miracles and she taught me to pray.

Pastor Russell Lee who brings me comfort.

Jim Holliday, for always being considerate and comforting to me.

Lynn Ellen Doxon saw the possibility in *Prayers from a Wounded Warrior* and gave me a chance to share my prayers with the world.

Brian Barnhart, my wonderful son and my joy.

PREFACE

I grew up in a home where God was never mentioned, the Bible never opened. In 1986, feeling that there was something more in the world I was drawn to go to church. This was my awakening to God. Three years later while finishing my Masters degree in health psychology I was diagnosed with mild Multiple Sclerosis. In 1995 the Internet blossomed and I discovered a website by Marianne Williamson, author of *A Return To Love*. On this website I found prayer requests from all over the world. Although I had never written prayers before, I, among others, replied to the requests. The human conditions and situations I was hearing were vast, so I chose to write a book on all subjects of prayer. The bulk of *Prayers From A Wounded Warrior* was written in the mid 1990's. The last prayer I wrote, "The Day the World Turned Upside Down", was a reflection on September eleventh.

In the late 1990's my MS galloped, or worsened. Two years ago I made the move from my home in California to New Mexico in order to be near my parents due to my worsening MS and the end of a long marriage. Little did I know that this move would lead me to people who would read these prayers and help me fulfill a ten year dream of publishing them.

This is a collection of prayers for our Hearts and Minds, Relationships, Bodies, Vocation, and the World. If your brow is furrowed with worry, fear or despair, may these prayers offer comfort, encouragement, and healing. It is my hope, that these prayers will soften your journey, making it easier and gentler.

If this is a time of celebration and things are going well, I join with you in prayers of gratitude, happiness and joy. May laughter fill your heart and spill over for all of us to share.

Let us join as one mind, heart and spirit as we travel on our journey together. I hope you enjoy these prayers as much as I enjoyed writing them. These prayers were written in first person so that the reader can identify with them. My wish is for you to make them your own.

Love,
Laura

Prayers From A Wounded Warrior

PRAYERS FOR OUR HEARTS AND MINDS

Letting Go and Letting God

Dear God,

*Revitalize my hope, restore my faith, and renew my
trust,*
May I remember here on earth there is always
The cycle of the seasons,
Cherry blossoms in the spring,
Thunderstorms,
A child being born,
A soul going Home,
Daybreak,
Moonlight,
Hearts opening with love,
People going separate ways,
Breaking ocean waves,
Water cutting rivers,
Scientific discoveries,
Molecules bonding,
Creative ideas bursting forth and coming to fruition,
Laughter and tears.

Dear God,
Remind me I need do nothing,
There is an underlying order to everything,
*May I let go and let You orchestrate divine
magnificence.*

Amen

Awakening Wonder

Dear God,

I have been numb and asleep,
Days pass and I forget to notice
>*moments of wonder and discovery.*

Renew and refresh all my senses.
May I once again appreciate
Colors at sunrise,
Clouds billowing across an azure sky,
Tender, green leaves budding on a once
>*dormant birch,*
Music beside a crackling hearth,
Aroma of freshly ground coffee,
Laughter shared with cherished friends,
Purring from a contented cat,
Gliding to slow music,
Walking after a fresh snowfall.

Remind me to open my eyes, ears, heart and mind,
To the splendor all around me.
Remind me that enjoyment and pleasure can be
found at any moment,
All I need do is look.

Amen

Relentless Change

Dear God,

There are so many changes in my life,
When I finally catch my breath, there is yet another
*   change.*
The hurricane seems relentless,
My mind, body and spirit feel shattered.

With your guidance,
May I be resilient in the storm,
Bend with the shifting wind,
Stand strong in the turbulence,
Listen for Your Voice above the chaos

I will gladly follow Your footsteps,
Sure in the knowledge
You are leading me out of the whirlwind.
Remind me, in your care, I am safe, never
*   comfortless, or alone.*
Dear God, with You as my guide, I am led to the
*   sanctuary within,*
Where peace, love, joy and strength eternally abide.

Amen

Anger

Dear God,

Sometimes I erupt like a volcano,
Molten lava spewing forth and harming all of those in
my path.
Sometimes I simmer and seethe, internally inflicting
discomfort.
Either way, Dear God, help me with this,
Show me a better way,
Let me see situations and people differently,
I relinquish my need to control,
I surrender always having to be right.

Calm my troubled mind,
Heal my raging heart,
Mend my shattered spirit,
Renew my fading faith,
Remind me that on the morrow, this too shall pass,
Let me relax and sink into the softness of Your
comforting arms.

Amen

Stress

Dear God,

I am wound in knots,
My muscles ache,
My mind is confused,
My stomach is in turmoil,
My heart beats out of rhythm.

Help me find balance and regain my bearings.
Remind me to let go of unnecessary tasks and
simplify my life.
Lead me to tranquil waters when the tide is low,
Caress my tired feet at the ocean's edge,
Massage my knotted shoulders with Your healing
touch, Lift me above my troubles.

I give you my stress, burdens and worries;
I give you my attachments to the past and future.
You know better than I what will bring me serenity,
peace and joy,
May I welcome the morning renewed, refreshed and
relaxed,
May I greet the new day, reborn.

Amen

Going With the Flow

I am tired of paddling up stream,
Getting caught in the rapids,
Circling around and around in an eddy.

Dear God, align me with Your will,
May I learn to trust You in every situation,
May I fulfill Your plan for my life.

Carry me Home,
Deliver me to You,
Let the water gently flow.

Amen

Depression

Dark clouds hover overhead,
Tears of sorrow streak my face,
Heaviness weighs me down,
I do not know where else to turn.

Dear God, heal my mind, heal my heart,
Part the clouds with Your radiant Light,
Dry the tears with Your powerful rays,
Lift my spirits with Your touch,
Give me new life.

May my spirit catch the updraft,
And soar on angel's wings
To the sacred alter within,
Where peace, joy and happiness are forever mine.

Amen

Grief

There has been a major loss in my life,
I feel empty and shattered,
Tears come easily.

Dear God,
Remind me the raw edges will soften with time,
Pain will lessen as days become months,
Memories will remain cherished keepsakes.

Heal my hurt,
Wipe my tears,
Carry me when I stumble,
Restore my hope,
Renew my spirit,
May I once again, greet the morning with promise.

Amen

Self Love

I feel so barren and worthless,
My inner landscape seems to be full of craters
          and scars,
Within a war rages,
I am my own worst enemy.

Dear God,
Purify all negative thoughts,
Cleanse me of self doubt, self hatred, unworthiness
          and guilt,
May I learn to accept and love myself the way I am.

Transform my mind into an inner landscape of a lush,
          green meadow,
Reflect in the eternal pool the light of a beautiful
          human being,
Me.

Amen

Judgment

I am quick to judge. Attacking something he said or something she did not do. My expectations of another are great and approval not easily given. I know when I judge another I attack myself. They are my thoughts that disrupt my internal calm, not theirs. It is my heart that beats and blood pressure rises.

Dear God,

Help me with this,
Open my mind, open my heart, and open my eyes,
Loft the veil of prejudice,
Show me how to look at the differences in another
*   with acceptance,*
Let me see others as my brother or sister,
Remind me that the past is over and tomorrow has
*   not arrived,*
Grant me peace through forgiving another,
Grant me peace through forgiving myself.

Let your strength overcome weakness,
Let Your light dispel shadows,
Let Your love transcend fear,
Let forgiveness reign,
With new sight, may judging others be of the past.

Amen

Self Doubt

Dear God,

Self doubt nibbles away. Uncertainty overwhelms. I question all of my actions.
Did I do the right thing, say the right words, respond fast enough?

I give You nagging speculations, that start with "what if",
I give You circular thoughts, that etch grooves in my mind,
I give You false assumptions, that never come to pass,
I give You the creases, embedded in my brow.

Calm my active mind,
Boost my self-confidence,
Help me stop doubting my actions and words,
Restore belief in myself,
Remind me to trust you.

Amen

Living In the Moment

Dear God,

I forget to acknowledge the blessings found today,
I have been living inside photographs of yesterday,
Possibilities of tomorrow that have not yet come.

When I yearn for a new beginning,
All I need to do is look at the world with fresh eyes,
Trust Your plan for my life,
Listen for Your Voice and Guidance,
May I remember, it is in the moment I am reborn.

Amen

Inner Strength

Dear God,

May I hear Your Voice above the tumultuous waves.
Lead me to peaceful shores,
Purify my spirit with salt air,
Renew my strength,
Revitalize my energy.

With You by my side,
I am resilient,
I am transformed,
I am empowered,
I am strong,
I am light.
I am Love.

Amen

Forgiveness

Dear God,

I feel remorse about my actions and behavior,
I feel regret about what I said I would do and didn't,
I anguish over the pain, I caused myself or another,
I am despondent over what I perceive are my failures.

Heal my mind,
Lighten my heavy heart,
Release the chains that hold me in bondage,
Rid me of internal pain,
Dissolve my binding guilt,
Remind me that yesterday is over,
Today I am free.

Amen

Forgiving Others

Dear God,

May I forgive her for what she said,
May I forgive him for what he did,
My heart is raw with pain,
I know my incessant thoughts of another's actions
        hold me in shackles.

Heal my thoughts,
Heal my pain,
Part the dark clouds that hover overhead,
May I know peace.

Lord,
There are some things done to another or others,
That are so atrocious, unthinkable,
Forgiveness seems remote, impossible.

In times like this,
Carry me across the chasm of confusion, despair, and
bewilderment.

Amen

Silence

My internal chatter is incessant. You gently speak to me, throughout the day and in my dreams at night. Dear God, I am ready to listen.

Dear God,
May I learn to sit in silence and hear only Your Voice,
May I learn to distinguish Your Voice from my own,
May my mind be emptied of wandering thoughts,
May my heart be calm and serene.

In silence, I hear your Voice,
In silence, I find inner peace,
In silence, I am centered,
In silence, I unite with You.

Amen

PRAYERS FOR OUR
RELATIONSHIPS

Friendship

Dear God,

You have blessed us with a sacred bond.
A cherished friend,
Who listens in my time of need,
Shares the joy of my accomplishments,
Offers a hug when good fortune knocks,
Stands by my side, when life becomes unsettled,
Reminds me to laugh, when I am too serious,
Offers guidance, when I need clarity,
Picks me up when I fall,
Calls when I am feeling alone,
Keeps my private affairs to her own counsel.
May we journey through life together,
Over peaks and through valleys,
Letting You lead our way.

Amen

Newborn

Our home had been blessed with a new babe,
Joy fills our hearts and sings the song of thanks,
Happiness lights our lives,
We are radiant.

His eyes mirror a world of gentle, innocence,
His touch softens our hearts,
His breath breathes the sweetest lullaby,
His love unites all souls.

Dear God, may you walk before him,
Protect him from harm,
May your angels carry our baby on soft,
        feathered wings,
Wrap him in arms which love eternally.

Amen

Children

Dear God,

I feel blessed to raise this precious child,
He brings such joy to our lives,
He has taught me to
See the world as magical and wondrous;
Everything new and awaiting discovery.

He finds happiness in
Chasing an illusive squirrel,
Swinging to reach the clouds,
Playing make-believe in the park,
Galloping like a pony in knee high grass.

Dear God,
He has taught me to keep life in perspective.
Through the eyes of innocence,
I am reborn, renewed and alive,
I am learning to once again play.

Amen

Teens

Dear God,

I surrender my parenthood to You,
Guide me in teaching my child to be honest,
        trustworthy and kind.

Teach me how to be strong, flexible and calm when
        challenges arise,
Let me know, when it is time to step forward and
        establish boundaries
or step back and keep my own counsel.

Protect and guide her always, so that she is not
        swayed by destructive influences.
May she grow into her own power and strength,
May she know that she is always a radiant beacon of
        light in my life, in all of our lives.

Dear God, protect and watch over our daughter.

Amen

Our Elders

Dear God,

A loved one is frail,
He experiences many physical ailments,
His mind wanders,
Walking has become difficult,
Days are spent in bed.

May his remaining days on earth be gentle,
His path softened by evening light,
When the autumn sun sets in the west,
And twilight colors wash the sky,
Remind me that our bond is forever sealed,
Love is eternal.

Amen

Attracting Love

Dear God,

My heart feels so empty,
The loneliness unbearable.
Please send me someone to share sorrow,
*   joy and love,*
The very threads that weave the tapestry of our lives.

May I hear a key in the door at the end of the day,
Familiar footsteps walking down the hall,
Voices conversing,
The sound of laughter.

Dear God, may I find someone to go
*   walking at sunset*
When homes are settling for the night,
May I find someone who shares my interests,
*   friends and family.*

Please join me in a sacred union with another,
Where we serve Your purpose,
Where we are beacons of Light for each other,
And hearts the world over.

Amen

Love For Him

I am in love,
My thoughts are only of him,
His heart is tender and true,
We are connected in mind, body and spirit,
In him, I see reflections of myself,
Together, we sing in joyous harmony,
Share a sacred bond.

Dear God, when trying times knock,
May we always remember to forgive one another,
Let go of resentment, guilt and pain,
Understand and accept our differences.

May the pleasing melody of a mountain stream
Sing a healing song,
Cleanse our troubles,
Revitalize our love,
May the water endlessly flow.

Amen

Love For Her

Dear God,

My beloved blesses me with tenderness,
Her laughter fills my heart,
Her gentleness smoothes rough edges,
Her beauty refreshes tired eyes,
Her honesty seals our bond.

Together, we dance for joy,
Discover reflections of ourselves,
Sing in unison,
Touch the God within,
As One we celebrate life.

Amen

Marriage

We join on this day in a sacred union,
Our hearts swell with love for each other,
Bringing us joy, happiness, and companionship,
We are committed to walk through life together as
one.

Remind us that when lightening strikes and
*   thunder rolls,*
On the horizon there will soon be a clear
*   cloudless sky,*
This is just a passing storm.

We agree to honor our vows,
In sickness and in health,
For better or for worse,
Till death do us part.

With you by our side, we are blessed and
*   surrounded with Your Light,*
Our star burns bright.

Amen

Separation

Dear God,

Our paths have diverged,
One sails west, one sails east,
We don't agree on anything,
Communication is nonexistent,
Disagreement has left us shattered.

The pain swallows my waking thoughts.
Nights are long.
My sadness is echoed by poor health,
I have lost my bearings,
I feel swept by a gale.

Still the tumultuous waters.
Give us strength to stay afloat.
Watch over our separate voyages.
May I forgive and sincerely wish him a safe journey,
May I genuinely forgive him for harsh words
*   and past hurts.*

Let me awake to the new day with anticipation
*   and joy,*
Lift my eyes to the expansive horizon.
I am ready to lower the mast,
Lead me safely to harbor.

Amen

Reconciliation

Dear God,

I am so lonely, though I live with someone.
Connecting with our hearts is nonexistent,
Communication is rare,
Though we share the same roof, we live in solitude.

Bridge the gap between us,
Dismantle the barriers that keep us apart,
Cleanse our past hurts,
Soften damaging words,
Restore the joy we once shared.

May we perceive our lives differently,
Show us a new path to follow,
Let us see our togetherness with fresh eyes,
May the barren slumber of winter pass,
And the arrival of spring offer renewal and rebirth.

Amen

Holidays

At this time of year, I feel fragmented, stressed and off balance. There is discord between families, finances are tight and a feeling of do more, buy more, smile more, pervades the air waves, the stores, and shouts at me from commercials. I am overwhelmed.

Dear God,

Please reawaken the childlike joy of celebration,
Rekindle my enthusiasm for festivities,
Heal ancient family wounds,
Help me surrender expectations,
Accept gifts graciously,
Renew faltering hope,
Absolve binding guilt,
Free me of passing judgments.

Let me remember to;
Give to a hungry family,
Wrap a cold child in a coat,
Wipe a tear of loneliness,
Invite a sister or brother to my dinner table,
Smile at an angry face.

May I join with hands and hearts around the world in
*   prayers for peace,*
May the flame of peace burn in every heart, every
home, on our streets and
*   between warring countries,*
May the flame illumine the world, and shine eternally.

Amen

Our Pets

Dear God,

Thank you for blessing my life with these
*   wonderful creatures,*
When the world appears to be upside down,
My furry friends, greet me with
Boundless energy,
Unconditional love,
Contented purring,
Wet kisses,
A call for stroking
Jumping in my lap,
Rubbing against my legs.

In their presence, I breathe out the day, focus on the
*   moment, smile and laugh.*
They reassure and remind, that life is simple, joyful
*   and blessed.*

Amen

PRAYERS FOR OUR BODIES

Restful Sleep

Dear God,

May I fall into a deep sleep tonight,
Cleansed of yesterdays troubles,
Free of tomorrow's worries.

May my dreams be peaceful, insightful and gentle,
May I sleep through the night without waking,
May I greet the new day refreshed and renewed.

May I awake, knowing my prayers will be answered,
May I awake, hopeful, calm and serene,
May I awake, grateful that I am alive.

Amen

An Ill Child

Dear God,

Our beloved child is not well,
Grant him a healing miracle
So he may run and play with the other boys and girls.
Part the heavens,
Vanish the cloud of illness.

Please, send Your angels to minister him,
When he is scared, may they hold his hand,
When he is in pain, gently wipe his tears,
When he is sad, sing to him,
When he is weak, embrace him with strength,
Let him fly on their wings to You,
In Your arms he is healed, he is whole, he is reborn.

Amen

Pain

Dear God,

Release me from the pain in my heart, mind,
        body and spirit,
Into Your open hands
I give You my bodily aches and pain,
I give You the open wounds that sear my heart,
I give You tears of sorrow that flow in the night,
I give You misperceptions seen with veiled eyes,
I give You disappointment.

Dear God,
Free me of this pain,
Lift me above the darkness,
To Your comforting arms,
Where I am carried in Love.

Amen

Recovery From Illness

Dear God,

I am very ill and frightened,
To Your divine hands, I surrender all thoughts of
worry, anxiety, doubt, and fear
about my illness,
May I stay open and receptive to all possible
channels for healing,
Lead me to the right healer, physician, medicine or
treatment.

Take my hand, as I travel this unknown road,
Restore my strength, renew my courage, reaffirm
my will to be well,
May I walk so close to You on my healing journey,
my footprints are Yours.
Dear God, heal my mind, heal my heart, heal my
spirit, heal me.

Amen

Transcending Illness

Dear God,

I have an illness that medicine and other healing
*   treatments have not abated or remitted,*
I am weary, worn and tired.

Dissolve my fear of uncertain future days,
Wrap me in Your protective arms,
Remind me, I am forever safe, protected and loved.

Divine Healer, mend my mind, soften my heart,
Give me the strength and courage to meet each day,
I am more than a body,
I am spirit,
I am light.

On Your powerful wings,
My soul transcends,
On Your powerful wings
I soar.

Amen

Healing For a Loved One

Dear God,

A loved one is very ill,
Days are spent in bed,
Nights are long,
He feels hopeless.

With each exhalation, may he rid himself at,
the cellular, metabolic,
biochemical and all levels,
debris that interferes with his well-being.
With each exhalation may he breathe out all
fearful thoughts that
constrict his mind, heart and spirit.

With each inhalation, may he breathe in Your
healing power,
With each inhalation, may hope be renewed,
With each inhalation, may strength be regained,
With each inhalation, may inner peace prevail.

With a grateful heart and loving thoughts,
I give thanks for his recovery,
In Your eyes, he is healed, he is whole.

Amen

Surgery

Dear God,

Soon, I will be admitted into the hospital for some
necessary surgery,
I am afraid of the results, the effect of the anesthesia
and if I will recover quickly.

I am frightened.
I turn this fear over to You.
Guide the surgeons hands with accuracy,
Surround the operation with Your healing light.
May the operation be successful, the recovery gentle,
Shine Your Light on all minds and hands during the
procedure.
I know that in Your care, I am safe and protected.

Dear God, give me strength, hope and peace,
Grant me a healing miracle.

Amen

Disability or Injury

Dear God,

I have become physically disabled,
Daily functions are challenged,
Mobility barriers loom,
Smiling is often an effort.

Surround me with Light,
Lift my heavy heart,
Show me how to rebuild my life,
Reveal my purpose.

Remind me, though I may have only one wing,
I can still fly,
Helped by others and carried by You,
On the wings of Love, I soar.

Amen

Caregivers

Dear God,

I have become dependent on another for the daily
needs of feeding, bathing and transportation,
You have blessed me with one who is loving, caring
and concerned for my well-being.

I am grateful for this dear one who
Attends to my basic needs,
Stays with me around the clock,
Offers a comforting smile when I feel discouraged,
Reassures with a kind word when hope fades.

Revitalize their energy when they feel exhausted,
Massage their shoulders when days and nights
*   are long,*
Send them relief when a change is welcomed,
May the scent of spring rain, cleanse, refresh and
renew.

Amen

When A Loved One Is Dying

Dear God,

Take this wonderful spirit to the ocean,
Wash away her fear of the unknown with each
           breaking wave,
Cleanse her heart with gentle waters,
Purify her spirit with sea air.

When the setting sun heralds dusk,
And majestic colors paint the sky,
Let her quietly slip from earth to heaven,
Welcomed by Your outstretched arms.

Amen

The Stairway Home
The death of a loved one

Dear God,

A dear one has made her transition Home,
In this time of mourning, wipe our tears,
Lighten our pain,
Carry the heaviness of our loss,
Remind us, her spirit is eternal.

May Your angels escort her in ascending the
stairway upward,
The hand hewn stairs, memories of lessons past,
May your angels
Receive her with glory,
Surround her with light,
Embrace her with love,
Celebrate her with joy,
Bless her with peace,
Deliver her to You.

Amen

LIFE PASSAGES

Aging

I am feeling and looking old,
In the mirror
There are more threads of gray,
Lines of deeper creases,
An aching body.

Dear God,

Remind me that with age comes wisdom,
confidence, strength and clarity.
That beauty is internal,
Radiated in a smile,
Spoken in a well-advised word,
Reflected in the sheen of aged patina,
that is lovingly polished over time,

Dear God, help me make wise choices,
So I may live life fully, untroubled and with integrity.
May I always listen for Your Voice,
May I heed Your signposts on my journey Home.

Amen

Empty Nest Syndrome

Dear God,

The house is now empty.
I miss the familiar sounds.
The rummaging in the refrigerator after a late night
       on the town,
cupboard doors banging,
the bathroom door creaking.
Knowing they are safely home,
I now can drift into a deep sleep.

They are now flying on their own wings,
May storms be only passing,
May their flight be gentle, rewarding, and enriching.

Protect them and guide them on their new journey.

Thank you,

Amen

PRAYERS FOR OUR VOCATIONS

Clarity

Dear God,

I feel so confused, and unfocused,
A dense fog, blocks my view.

Lift the mist before my eyes,
Roll the fog out to sea,
Shine with crystal clarity, Your plan for my life.
May it unfold with the ebb and flow of each wave,
May doubt and confusion sink with the setting sun,
May the Northern Star guide me on my
         appointed path,
May I sail effortlessly on uncharted seas.

I surrender my need to control,
I surrender my expectations.
Align me with Your will,
Bless me with clear eyes, new vision,
Your vision for my voyage home.

Amen

My Calling

Dear God,

Why was I born?
What is my calling?
How can I make a decent living doing what I enjoy?
How do I find meaningful work?

Please reveal to me my purpose,
Reveal my unique gifts, talents and abilities,
Reveal to me my barriers to them, so I may make amends.

I surrender my goals, for You know, what is best,
I surrender my feelings of doubt and inadequacy,
I surrender my illusions that hold me back.

May my work be like slipping on a comfortable pair of shoes.
May I walk with clear intention and direction knowing with certainty
That I am walking in the right direction,
May I be accomplished and receive the rewards of success.
Use me, so I may be an instrument for your highest good.

Amen

Treading Water

I feel like I am treading water. I am neither going backward or forward. I travel congested freeways up and down in heavy traffic. My salary barely covers the bills, sometimes not all. I worry about my family. I worry about our future. I worry about my health. I worry about me. I worry about everything.

Dear God,

I am tired of worrying,
Wipe the worry from my brow,
Take the heavy burden off my shoulders,
Lift me above the clouds of discontent.

Bless me with new eyes, so I may see differently,
Show me a better way, a new path to follow,
I relinquish my plans,
In gratitude, I accept Your vision,
Align me with Your Will.

Amen

Money

I feel so inadequate around money. There never seems to be enough. I fear money. I give up my power, good sense and ability to manage it properly. Money controls me. I live in the illusion of lack. The consequences are physically, mentally and emotionally great.

Dear God,

Help me with this,
I know, money holds no power,
It is only a tool to meet my needs, desires and better
*   the lives of those who have less.*
Through right action, may I become an able steward
*   of money.*

Remind me, that what I do well, will bring meaning,
*   satisfaction, prosperity and serve others,*
Lead me in the right direction, where to go, whom to
*   speak to and what to say,*
Bless me with new and creative ideas,
Sow an idea in my mind, that when planted and
tended, will come to fruition like
*   an orchard at harvest.*

Amen

PRAYERS FOR OUR WORLD

The Day The World Turned Upside Down
A reflection on September 11

Dear God,

I am confused.
I don't understand the ill will, destruction, and terror
directed towards nations of the free world, especially
my own. My world as I once knew it was shattered.
Shards of broken glass, painful memories of a
catastrophic day, now remind us to be cautious, on
guard, alert.

But, there was an outpouring of concern, help,
         and prayers,
Healing came from hearts and hands around the
         world that joined together as one,
Your Light dispelled the darkness that blanketed us,
We witnessed the power of Love, Your presence.

Thank you,

Amen

Creatures Large and Small

Dear God,

You have blessed us with creatures large and small,
On land, in our oceans, lakes and air,
Each an essential thread in Your intricate and
magnificent food web.

Many are now extinct.
Daily, more are becoming only a memory.
Urgently, I ask You to intercede and transform human
minds all over the world.

Through prayer, right thinking and positive action,
guide us as guardians and stewards of the earth,
May our children and those unborn, know a world
where all creatures have a rightful place in Your
kingdom.

May we respond with haste.

Amen

The Earth

Dear God,

May the assault and scourge of our precious earth by
> *toxins,*
> *pollution,*
> *cutting the rain forests*
> *and other environmental hazards,*

change through prayer,
> *responsible action,*
> *laws that protect,*
> *and leadership that cares.*

Transform minds everywhere, so we may collectively act and not complain about the condition of our planet.

Remind us, dear Lord,
We are stewards of the planet,
We are responsible for the children and those unborn,
We are in charge of plants and animals,
We are the trustees of minerals, soil and air.
Teach us to be responsive,
Give us wisdom.

May we act with trustworthy intention.
Shake us from our slumber,
Awaken us.

Amen

World Peace

Dear God,

May peace prevail on earth
Between countries at war,
People of different religions, colors, and cultures,
On our streets,
In our homes,
In our hearts and minds.

Grant us the wisdom to make amends.
Turn wrongs into responsible action,
Find solid solutions,
Restore shattered cities,
Heal severed bonds,
Forgive terrible acts done to our brothers,
Resolve ancient hatreds.

Guide us in building a bridge across boundaries
*   and nations,*
Uniting people of all colors, religions, and cultures,
May we celebrate our diversity,
And fly with the Dove of Peace,
Joining You in spreading Love throughout the world.

Amen

GRATITUDE

Prayer of Gratitude

Dear God,

Your signature is everywhere,
Painted across the majestic outdoors,
Waterfalls cascading to the valley below,
Granite peaks ascending skyward,
Ocean waves rushing to the shore,
Wildflowers showering a spring meadow.

Your presence is heard in the laughter of children
    at play,
Seen in the knowing twinkle of an elder's eye,
Shared in the embrace of a cherished friend,
Reflected in the smile of a stranger on a winter
    morning,
Felt in a circle of hands before a meal.

Your Voice gently whispers to us when life appears
    fragmented,
And fear, sorrow, frustration and depression descend,
On Your shoulders, our heavy knapsack is carried,
In Your arms, we rest safe, protected and comforted.

Thank you for answering our prayers,
Thank you for healing our minds, hearts, bodies and
    spirits,
Thank you for the mystery of the Infinite.

Amen

CELEBRATING THE LIGHT

Celebrating The Light

Dear God,

There is a circle of dark clouds in my mind,
The clouds are damp with yesterday's thoughts,
Heavy with tomorrow's worries,
My view is obscured by an opaque mist before my
eyes.

With You as my Guide,
Lead me through the clouds to my inner Light,
Renew, refresh, and rejuvenate every cell of my body,
Cleanse every shadowed thought in my mind.

In Your Light may I celebrate my inner strength,
beauty, and true self.
In gratitude I accept Your Grace.

Amen

About the Author:

Laura Barnhart has worked in education and as a motivational speaker. She holds a Master's in health psychology and lectured on topics such as stress management and interpersonal communication. In 1979 she married Bill Barnhart and their only son, Brian, was born in 1984.

She was raised in the Bay area of California, in a home without God or any Biblical teaching. As an adult she began searching for meaning. Her search led her to church, where she became a Christian. Shortly after, she began writing the prayers in this book in response to prayer requests on the Internet. She responded compassionately to the needs of people in all walks of life, with widely varying needs and situations.

In 1989 Laura was diagnosed with Multiple Sclerosis. In 2001, in response to the worsening of her MS, her husband divorced her. The next year Laura moved into a nursing home in Albuquerque, New Mexico to be closer to her parents and a new church community where she has gotten the care she needed. Today, although Laura's voice is failing, her writing continues to lead and inspire us.

Also available from Artemesia Publishing!

Rainbows from Heaven
by Lynn Ellen Doxon

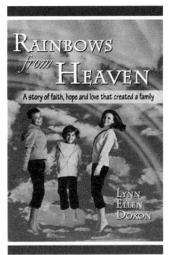

Families are made in Heaven.

That was never so apparent as it was for Lynn Ellen Doxon and Robert Habiger in the creation of their family through the adoption of Anastasia, Janalyn, and Lydia. Lynn and Robert's journey takes them halfway around the world to Ukraine, and lasts for two and a half years. In that time they learn lessons of perseverance, faith, love, hope and surrender to God's will.

Lynn describes how a couple grew in ways they never expected when they set out to adopt just one unwanted child, how three beautiful girls found their family, and how one region of Ukraine was opened up to foreign adoption despite fearsome opposition.

Lynn shares the humor, the joy, the fear and the anger she experiences in the process of adopting her daughters. She opens herself up, showing that while she and Robert did not do everything right, continued trust in each other, prayer and belief in their love for the girls would see Lynn's dream of a family come true.

"...an inspirational story of boundless faith."
Sherry Russell – Midwest Book Review

Available in paperback or hardback.
Paperback: ISBN 1-932926-99-2 $14.95
Hardback: ISBN 1-932926-98-4 $24.95

Order your copy today from our website:
www.artemesiapublishing.com
or write us at: Artemesia Publishing
PO Box 6508
Rocky Mount, NC 27802-6508

Order Form

Prayers from a Wounded Warrior
Laura Barnhart

Order additional copies of this book for friends, family, and those in search of God's prayers and wisdom. Perfect for prayer groups, church missions, and celebrating events in your life.

Artemesia Publishing
12101 Palomas Ave, NE
Albuquerque, NM 87122
505-821-2808

Name: _____

Address: _____

_____

Telephone: _____

Quantity   Price   Total

_____ Prayers from a Wounded Warrior $9.95   _____
        (ISBN 1-932926-31-3)
                             Total Due: _____

(Send no payment, we will send you an invoice with your order.)

Thank you for your order. God Bless.

Visit us on the web at: www.artemesiapublishing.com